This Book Belongs to:

A NEW BURLINGTON BOOK
The Old Brewery
6 Blundell Street
London N7 9BH

Consultant: Fiona Moss, RE Adviser at RE Today Services
Editor: Cathy Jones
Designer: Chris Fraser

Copyright © QEB Publishing, Inc. 2013

First published in the United States in 2013 by
QEB Publishing, Inc.
3 Wrigley, Suite A
Irvine, CA 92618

www.qed-publishing.co.uk

A CIP record for this book is available from the Library of Congress.

ISBN 978 1 60992 577 2

Printed in China

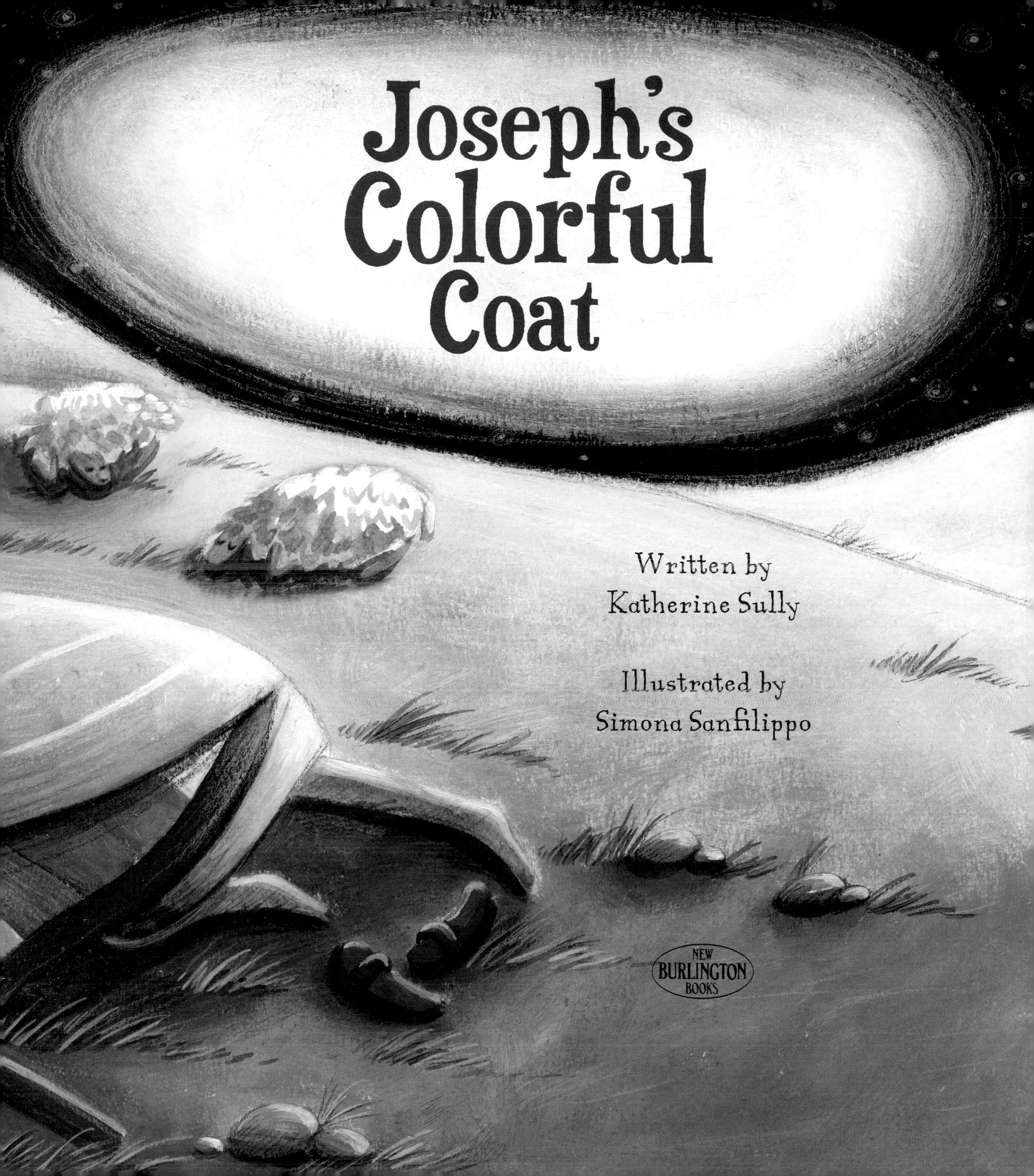

Joseph's Colorful Coat

Written by
Katherine Sully

Illustrated by
Simona Sanfilippo

NEW
BURLINGTON
BOOKS

Long ago, Joseph's father, Jacob,
gave him a colorful new coat.
This made Joseph's brothers angry.

Joseph was younger
than his eleven brothers.

"Why does he get a new coat and we don't?" grumbled one brother.

"He's always the favorite," complained another.

One night, Joseph had two dreams.

In the first dream, eleven bundles of wheat gathered around Joseph's bundle and bowed.

Snore! Snore!

In the second dream, the sun, moon, and eleven stars bowed to Joseph.

When Joseph told his brothers about the dreams, they were angry.

"Do you think we are going to bow to you?" they asked.

Soon after, Joseph went to find his brothers.
They were still annoyed with him. When they saw
him coming, they said,
"Let's kill him and pretend a
wild animal attacked him."

But brother Reuben tried to save him.
"Let's just leave him in this empty well.
If we tear his coat, Father will think he is dead."

Just then, some merchants
came riding by with camels.
They were on their way to Egypt.

Brother Judah hatched another plan.
"Let's sell Joseph to the merchants as a slave."

And that's what they did.

The brothers went home and showed their father Joseph's torn coat. Jacob thought that Joseph was dead. He was very sad.

But Joseph was on his way to Egypt to be sold as a slave.

Joseph became a slave of one of the king's officers. For a long time he was happy and trusted by his master.

But the master's wife tricked him and he went to jail.

Two men were in the jail with Joseph.

The first man said, "I had a dream—what does it mean? I squeezed three grapevines into the king's cup."

Joseph said happily, "God knows what your dream means. In three days, the king will send for you to be his wine servant."

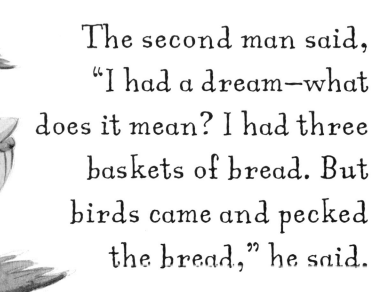

The second man said, "I had a dream—what does it mean? I had three baskets of bread. But birds came and pecked the bread," he said.

Joseph said sadly, "God knows what your dream means. In three days you will die."

Both dreams came true.

Then, one day, the king had two dreams. In the first dream, seven skinny cows ate seven fat cows!

In the second dream, seven straggly cornstalks ate seven strong cornstalks!

Snore! Snore!

When the king told his dreams to the
wise men, they were puzzled.

But then the king's wine servant said,
"I know someone who can tell you what your
dreams mean. His name is Joseph."

The king sent for Joseph. He said: "I had two dreams—what do they mean?" And he told Joseph his dreams.

Joseph said, "God knows what your dreams mean.

Seven fat cows and seven strong cornstalks mean seven years of good harvest.

Seven skinny cows and seven straggly cornstalks mean seven years of bad harvest."

"Oh, no! What will we do?" asked the king.

"Save wheat from the good harvest to feed the people during the bad harvest," said Joseph.

The king was so pleased that
he put Joseph in charge.

For seven years the harvest was
good, and they kept some wheat.

For the next seven years the harvest was bad,
but the people had plenty to eat.

Far away, Joseph's father and brothers were hungry.
"Oh, no! What will we do?" they cried.

"We will go to Egypt—they have
plenty of food," said Jacob.

After a long journey, Jacob and the brothers arrived in Egypt. They bowed down before the man in charge of food.

Imagine their surprise when they looked up and saw Joseph!

Joseph was pleased to see his father and brothers after all these years. The dream he had had all those years ago had come true.

Next Steps

Look back through the book to find more to talk about and join in with.

★ Copy the actions. Be a bundle of wheat bowing down, or be a twinkling star.

★ Join in with the rhyme. Pause to encourage joining in with "I had a dream—what does it mean?"

★ Counting. Count three vines, three baskets, seven fat cows, seven skinny cows, seven strong cornstalks, seven straggly cornstalks, eleven brothers, eleven bundles of wheat, eleven stars.

★ Colorful coat: name the colors in the coat together, then look back to spot the colors on other pages.

★ All shapes and sizes: describe the brothers in terms of shape or size, looking for a tall brother, a short brother, a fat brother, a thin brother.

★ Listening: when you see the word on the page, point, and make the sound—Snore!

Now that you've read the story...what do you remember?

★ Who was Joseph?
★ Why did his brothers leave Joseph in the well?
★ Where did the merchants take Joseph?
★ What happened to Joseph in Egypt?
★ How did he get out of jail?
★ When Joseph saw his father and brothers, how did he feel?

What does the story tell us?
God has a plan for all of us if we listen to Him.